Silhouettes and Shadows: Stories of Soul and Strife

Jassila Sikkandar

BookLeaf Publishing
India | USA | UK

Presentation by *BookLeaf Publishing*

Web: www.bookleafpub.com

E-mail: info@bookleafpub.com

ISBN: 9789363315853

First edition 2024

To those who find solace in the written word, and to those who seek truth within the lines of verse:

This book is dedicated to the dreamers who look beyond the surface, to the seekers who embrace the journey of self-discovery, and to the hearts that find comfort in poetry's embrace.

May these poems resonate with your own experiences, illuminate the shadows of your thoughts, and inspire the beauty within.

With gratitude and hope,

Jassila Sikkandar

ACKNOWLEDGEMENT

As I reflect on the creation of Silhouettes and Shadows: Stories of Soul and Strife, my foremost gratitude goes to the Almighty. It is through divine guidance and inspiration that this collection has materialized, and I am deeply appreciative of the myriad of support and encouragement that has made this journey possible.

To my daughter Sana and my family, your inspiration and unwavering support have been a constant source of strength.

To my editor and publishing team, your dedication and meticulous care have transformed my manuscript into a polished and cohesive collection. Your professionalism and creative insights have turned this book into a reality, and I am profoundly grateful for your hard work and commitment.

I also wish to extend my heartfelt thanks to the poets and writers who have influenced and inspired me. Your work has been a wellspring of creativity and personal enrichment, and through your example, I have discovered my own voice and passion for poetry.

To the readers who embark on this journey through the diverse landscapes of verse, thank you for engaging with this book. Your connection to these poems is the ultimate reward for my efforts, and I hope that these verses resonate with you in meaningful ways.

Finally, I acknowledge the boundless world of poetry itself, which continues to inspire and challenge me. To this ever-evolving realm, I dedicate this collection, hoping it adds a meaningful shade to the rich fabric of poetic expression.

Thank you all for your invaluable support and for being a part of this poetic adventure.

With deep appreciation,
Jassila Sikkandar

PREFACE

Welcome to "Silhouettes and Shadows: Stories of Soul and Strife": a collection that ventures into the boundless expanse of human experience through the art of poetry. As the title suggests, this book is a vibrant mosaic of emotions, themes, and reflections, each poem a brushstroke on the canvas of contemporary life.

In crafting this anthology, I aimed to capture the kaleidoscope of our modern existence, exploring the myriad hues of love, loss, and longing, as well as the shadows cast by human tragedy and the dawn of personal growth. Through seventy distinct poems, I invite you to journey with me through the spectrum of human emotion and thought.

"Silhouettes and Shadows: Stories of Soul and Strife" is a collection born from a deep reverence for these fleeting treasures. Within these pages, you will find a tapestry of poems that seek to capture the ephemeral nature of life—moments that shimmer like dewdrops on morning petals, moments that whisper like the breeze through autumn leaves, moments that linger in the heart long after they have passed.

Each poem in this anthology is a reflection of personal encounters with life's fleeting beauty—inspired by the colors of a sunset, the fragrance of a blooming flower, or the touch of a loved one's hand. They are an invitation to pause, to breathe deeply, and to embrace the magic woven into the fabric of everyday existence.

Contemporary Life sets the stage, immersing readers in the rhythm and pulse of our digital age and urban existence. Here, the interplay between connection and solitude forms a backdrop for a deeper exploration of our times.

As we transition into the realm of **Love**, the poems unravel the complexities of affection, desire, and unspoken sentiments. These verses capture the essence of romantic connection and the heart's yearning, painting a portrait of love in all its facets.

Death brings us face-to-face with mortality, offering contemplative reflections on the end of life and the legacy we leave behind. These poems provide solace and provoke thought, challenging us to reconcile with the inevitable.

In the sections dedicated to **Grief, Loss, and Longing**, the poems delve into the profound sorrow and yearning that follow personal loss. Through these verses, I hope to provide a mirror for those navigating their own journeys through grief and memory.

Human Tragedy explores the darker side of our nature, addressing themes of betrayal, corruption, and cruelty. These poems confront the harsh realities of our world, reflecting on the moral and existential challenges we face.

The **Primordial Verse** section invites readers to connect with the ancient echoes that resonate within us all. These poems tap into the timeless rhythms of human existence, invoking the elemental forces that have shaped our collective heritage.

With **Techno Poetry**, the collection bridges the gap between tradition and modernity. These poems explore the impact of technology on our lives and language, blending contemporary themes with poetic expression.

Humor provides a refreshing counterpoint in the anthology. The **Humor** section offers a series of witty and whimsical poems, providing a lighthearted respite from the more intense themes.

The poems on **Irrationality, Obsession, and Paranoia** delve into the enigmatic corners of the mind. These pieces explore the boundaries between reality and delusion, capturing the essence of psychological turmoil and obsession.

Finally, **Personal Growth and Reflection** bring the journey full circle, celebrating the transformative power of self-awareness and personal evolution. These poems reflect on the process of change and the quest for inner clarity.

As you turn the pages of "*Silhouettes and Shadows: Stories of Soul and Strife,"* I hope you find resonance in these diverse voices and perspectives. Each poem is a window into a different facet of our shared human experience, inviting you to reflect, question, and connect with the depth of our collective journey.
Thank you for joining me on this poetic voyage.

May you find inspiration, solace, and insight within these fifty shades of verse.

With heartfelt gratitude,
Jassila Sikkandar

Ephemeral Moments

Morning Dew

Morning dew on blades of green,
Glistens with a gentle sheen,
Tiny pearls on grassy tips,
Nature's kiss in dawn's eclipse.

Whispers of the night's embrace,
Silent tears on petals lace,
New day's promise, fresh and true,
Morning dew, a world renewed

Butterfly Ballet

In gardens kissed by morning light,
Butterfly wings take flight,
Their dance a ballet of pure delight,
In nature's symphony, so bright.

Delicate wings, a vibrant hue,
Painting skies of azure blue,
A fleeting beauty, ever true,
In moments caught, they renew.

Each fluttering wing, a gentle sigh,
Whispering secrets as they fly,
Embracing life as time slips by,
In nature's dance, where dreams arise.

Oh, butterfly, ephemeral and free,
Your grace is a gift for all to see,
In your flight, we find the key,
To cherish life's brevity.

So let us dance as butterflies do,
In the waltz that nature brews,
Celebrating moments, old and new,
In fleeting beauty, forever true.

Sunset's Embrace

Sun dips low, paints the sky's canvas wide,
Colors blend, a fleeting tide,
Ephemeral hues in twilight's flight,
Sunset's embrace, a gentle delight.

Golden rays caress the earth,
Moments of magic, a fleeting birth,
Dancing clouds in crimson lace,
Painting the heavens with grace.

Whispers of day bid adieu,
As night unfolds its velvet hue,
Stars awaken, a sparkling start,
In twilight's glow, life's beating heart.

For in each sunset's fading gleam,
We find the beauty of life's dream,
A reminder that moments depart,
But in memory, they remain art.

Whispering Breeze

In the hush of twilight's grace,
Where the world slows its frantic pace,
Whispering breeze, so soft and light,
Paints the evening with gentle might.

Through the leaves, it weaves its tale,
Of distant lands and hidden trails,
Caressing meadows with tender sighs,
Underneath the darkening skies.

It carries secrets from afar,
Of ancient stars and dreams that spar,
Whispering words of love and woe,
In a language only zephyrs know.

Softly touching every tree,
Swaying branches in symphony,
It whispers hope to hearts that grieve,
And in its touch, we find reprieve.

Oh, whispering breeze, so pure and kind,
With your touch, tranquility we find,
Lifting burdens, calming seas,
In your whispers, we find peace.

Ocean's Lullaby

In the cradle of the endless sea,
Where waves whisper tranquility,
Ocean's lullaby begins to play,
Underneath the sun's golden ray.

Soft caresses of the salty breeze,
Echoing through the dancing seas,
Gentle rhythms of ebb and flow,
In the heart of the ocean's glow.

Whispers carried on the tide,
Secrets of the deep inside,
Mysteries woven in the foam,
Where ancient waters find their home.

Moonlight paints a silver trail,
Upon the waves, a shimmering veil,
Stars above like diamonds gleam,
In the ocean's eternal dream.

Sands of time shift silently,
Beneath the vast, eternal sea,
Ocean's lullaby, a timeless song,
In its embrace, we all belong.

Close your eyes, let worries fade,
In the cradle where dreams are made,
Ocean's lullaby, serene and wide,
Guides you gently with the tide.

Raindrop Serenade

In the silence of a rainy night's embrace,
Where each raindrop whispers with grace,
A serenade unfolds from heavens high,
Nature's orchestra, painting the sky.

Each drop a note in this symphony rare,
Tapping gently on the earth with care,
Melodies of liquid silver cascade,
Echoes of peace in the quiet they've made.

Soft rhythms dance on leaves and glass,
Pitter-patter, moments fleeting yet vast,
A lullaby sung to the sleeping land,
In every raindrop, a touch so grand.

From rooftops to rivers, a timeless song,
Nature's poetry, pure and strong,
Listen closely, let the serenade unfold,
Raindrops whisper secrets untold.

In the stillness of a rain-washed night,
Hearts find solace, souls take flight,
For in every drop that kisses the ground,
A serenade of peace is found.

Cherry Blossoms

Amidst the orchard, a soft caress,
Cherry blossoms in their dress,
Whispering secrets to the breeze,
Painting the air with fragrant ease.

Delicate petals, pale and fair,
Adorn the branches, a fleeting affair,
Each bloom a symbol, brief and bright,
Of nature's joy, of life's respite.

In the quiet of the early morn,
Their beauty shines, newly born,
A symphony of pink and white,
A gentle kiss of pure delight.

Underneath their blossomed crown,
Weary souls find solace found,
For in their presence, troubles cease,
And hearts are filled with tranquil peace.

Cherry blossoms, fleeting bloom,
Remind us of life's fragile loom,
Of moments cherished, passing by,
Underneath the azure sky.

In their bloom, a lesson found,
To savor beauty all around,
For like these blossoms, we too may,
In fleeting splendor, fade away.

Yet in our hearts, their memory gleams,
Cherry blossoms, in our dreams,
Forever cherished, forever known,
In whispered winds, their beauty shown.

Starry Night

Under the velvet canopy of night,
Where stars ignite their gentle light,
A painter's brush of cosmic hue,
Unveils a masterpiece anew.

Starry night, a tranquil sea,
Where dreams and wonders wander free,
Each twinkle tells a tale untold,
Of galaxies and mysteries bold.

Silent whispers in the dark,
Echoes of a celestial spark,
Nebulas swirl in mystic dance,
Infinite realms of circumstance.

Moonlight spills on fields below,
Where lovers' hearts in rhythm flow,
A symphony of quiet grace,
In this vast and boundless space.

Starry night, enchanting sight,
A canvas vast, a timeless flight,
In awe we gaze, our souls take flight,
In the embrace of a starry night

Autumn's Leaves

Autumn's leaves in gentle flight,
Whispering secrets of the night,
Golden, red, and amber too,
Painting skies with every hue.

Fluttering down from branches high,
Like nature's tears from a somber sky,
A carpet soft upon the ground,
In whispered rustles, they surround.

Each leaf a story, softly told,
Of summer's warmth now growing cold,
But in their fall, a beauty found,
In every sight and every sound.

They dance upon the playful breeze,
Their journey marked by whims and ease,
A fleeting dance, a final gleam,
Before they rest, in nature's dream.

In piles they gather, crisp and neat,
A tapestry laid at autumn's feet,
A mosaic of memories past,
In autumn's leaves, a spell is cast.

So let us walk amidst this grace,
Among the leaves in this tranquil place,
And feel the essence of the season,
In autumn's leaves, a whispered reason.

Snowflake's Kiss

In silent realms where winter weaves,
Snowflakes descend like whispered leaves.
Each one a crystal, uniquely spun,
In frosty air beneath the sun.

Softly they land with gentle grace,
A kiss upon the earth's embrace.
Tiny dancers in the cold,
Their beauty timeless, never old.

In every flake, a story told,
Of journeys far and dreams untold.
They paint the world in shimmering white,
A blanket woven through the night.

Each snowflake's kiss, a fleeting art,
A touch that warms the coldest heart.
In frosty stillness, pure and bright,
They sparkle, dance, and take flight.

So let us pause and watch them fall,
Each snowflake's kiss, a wonder small.
In winter's tale of blissful mirth,
They whisper secrets of the earth.

Ephemeral Moments, like snowflakes' embrace,
Remind us of life's fleeting grace,
In the chill of winter's fleeting kiss,
We find the beauty in moments like this.

For just as snowflakes kiss the ground,
So do moments in time swiftly pass,
Cherish each fleeting sight and sound,
For they, like snowflakes, won't forever last.

So let us hold dear these fragile things,
The moments that make our spirits sing,
For in their brief and wondrous flight,
We find the truest joy, pure and bright.

Firefly Glow

Amidst the twilight's gentle whispered hush,
Where day's last ember meets the coming night,
A firefly emerges from the hidden brush,
Its glow a beacon, a celestial light.

In fields aglow with the warmth of summer's breath,
It dances, flickers, a waltz in the air,
A tiny star born from the earth's sweet depth,
A fleeting magic, beyond all compare.

Oh, firefly, your luminescent grace,
A symphony of secrets you unfold,
In every flicker, a serene embrace,
A tale of wonder that will ne'er grow old.

So let us cherish this nocturnal show,
Where fireflies in their dance softly glow.

Misty Morning

Petals in the wind, a soft ballet of grace,
Drifting from the garden's embrace,
Carried by whispers of the zephyr's breath,
Dancing through the air, defying death.

Each petal, a fragment of a story told,
Of love's tender touch, both young and old,
They flutter and fall, like dreams untold,
In the gentle breeze, their journey unfolds.

Roses blush and lilies sigh,
Their petals scatter, bid goodbye,
To the bloom of spring, the warmth of sun,
Yet in their fall, a life begun.

They adorn the earth with fleeting grace,
A fragrant symphony in every place,
Silent witnesses to time's gentle flow,
Petals in the wind, they come and they go.

For even in their fleeting flight,
Petals paint the world with light,
A reminder of beauty in transient form,
In the wind they dance, weathering storm.

So cherish each moment, tender and kind,
Like petals in the wind, a treasure to find,
In their fragility, a lesson profound,
Life's fleeting beauty, forever unbound.

Gilded Horizon

Upon the gilded horizon, where day meets night,
A realm of magic and wonder takes flight,
Golden hues stretch across the expanse so wide,
Where dreams weave and dance with the tide.

Each sunset, a masterpiece painted with fire,
Igniting the heavens, igniting desire,
Whispers of promise in the fading light,
A canvas of hope, a canvas so bright.

In the quiet of twilight, dreams come alive,
In the heart's gentle rhythm, hopes strive,
Where the ocean meets the sky's endless bend,
A symphony of beauty without an end.

Oh, gilded horizon, enchantment untold,
Where mysteries linger, where stories unfold,
Guide us through shadows, guide us to grace,
In the embrace of your golden embrace.

For in every sunset, a new dawn is born,
In every horizon, a promise sworn,
To chase the light, to embrace the unknown,
In the gilded horizon, we find our home.

Echoes of Majesty

In mountains' majesty, where eagles dare to fly,
Where granite peaks scrape the azure sky.
Silent giants standing strong and tall,
Guardians of wilderness, they enthrall.

Their slopes adorned with blankets of green,
And icy streams that sparkle and gleam.
Whispering pines sway in the gentle breeze,
While echoes of legends linger with ease.

Snow-capped summits kissed by the dawn,
A haven for creatures, dusk until morn.
In every crevice, a story untold,
Of resilience and beauty, ageless and bold.

Majesty in solitude, a timeless scene,
Where earth meets heaven in a grand serene.
Mountains' majesty, a beacon of grace,
A sanctuary where spirits find their place.

Moonlit Reverie

In the hush of night, when stars ignite,
A moonlit reverie takes flight,
Silver beams weave through the trees,
Whispering secrets on the breeze.

The world bathed in a gentle glow,
Where dreams in shadows ebb and flow,
Each leaf a dancer, each flower a muse,
Under the spell of the moon's soft fuse.

A tranquil lake mirrors the night,
Reflecting the celestial light,
As thoughts unfurl in silent grace,
Lost in this enchanted space.

Oh, moonlit reverie, profound and deep,
In your embrace, the soul does steep,
In dreams that shimmer, in visions bright,
Guided by your tender light.

And as the night begins to wane,
The moonlit reverie remains,
A fleeting glimpse, a cherished sight,
Until we meet again, goodnight.

River's Reflection

In the gentle embrace of dusk's quiet sigh,
Where whispers of time with the river lie,
I see a mirror of the heavens above,
A canvas of dreams, mirrored with love.

The river's reflection, a shimmering dance,
Captures the sun's last golden glance,
Each ripple a story, each wave a tale,
Of mysteries deep, where secrets prevail.

Silent witness to the passage of years,
Flowing through laughter, flowing through tears,
It mirrors the moon in its silvery glow,
Reflecting the past, yet letting it go.

In its depths, I see shadows of trees,
Echoes of birdsong, carried by breeze,
A mosaic of colors, from dawn to night,
Painted with stars, reflecting their light.

O river of time, ceaselessly flowing,
Your mirror-like surface, softly glowing,
Hold within you the wonders untold,
In your reflection, mysteries unfold.

So I stand by your side, lost in your view,
As you whisper to me tales old and new,
And I learn from your wisdom, silent and deep,
In your river's reflection, my soul finds its keep.

Birdsong's Tale

In the quiet morn, where shadows fade,
Amidst the branches, a serenade,
Birdsong's tale in soft refrain,
Echoes of a world untamed.

From the sparrow's trill so sweet,
To the hawk's cry, fierce and fleet,
Each note, a lyric, pure and clear,
Telling tales both far and near.

Through forest dense and meadow wide,
Where ancient rhythms softly glide,
Winged choristers, poets bold,
Craft their stories, manifold.

They sing of journeys through the skies,
Of dawn's embrace and twilight's sighs,
Of nests adorned with tender care,
And dreams that linger in the air.

Birdsong's tale, a timeless art,
A symphony that stirs the heart,
In every warble, every trill,
Nature's song is echoing still.

Twilight's Hush

In twilight's hush, the world turns still,
Whispers of evening softly spill.
A palette of dusk paints the sky,
Where day and night in quiet lie.

The trees, they sway in gentle breeze,
Their leaves a rustling symphony.
The stars above begin to peep,
Through velvety night's embrace deep.

In twilight's hush, a moment's grace,
Where time suspends in a tranquil space.
The cares of day now fade away,
As shadows lengthen and gently sway.

A moonbeam casts its silver gleam,
Upon the waters, calm and serene.
Reflecting dreams of distant shores,
In twilight's hush, the heart explores.

Silent echoes of the day now past,
In twilight's hush, they softly last.
A fleeting hour, a peaceful sigh,
Underneath the vast, darkening sky.

So let us linger, just a while,
In twilight's hush, where thoughts beguile.
And let the world slip out of sight,
In this serene and quiet night.

Whispers of Spring

In whispers soft, the earth awakes,
From winter's slumber, it shakes and breaks.
Beneath the thawing frost and snow,
Life stirs with a gentle, hopeful glow.

The crocus blooms with a purple hue,
A herald of the season new.
Its petals unfurl to greet the sun,
A dance of warmth just begun.

Birdsong fills the morning air,
As melodies of joy declare
That spring has come with tender grace,
To paint the world in a vibrant embrace.

The scent of blossoms in the breeze,
From cherry trees to apple seas.
Each petal whispers secrets bright,
Of longer days and softer light.

Fields of green stretch endlessly,
Awakening from wintry sleep.
In whispers of spring, we find our voice,
To celebrate life and rejoice.

Oh, whispers of spring, so sweet and clear,
Your promise of renewal we hold dear.
In every bud and every wing,
We hear the song that you bring.

Wandering Clouds

In skies of blue, where dreams unfurl,
Wandering clouds, like sails they swirl,
Drifting on a breath of breeze,
Stories whispered through the trees.

Softly floating, weightless flight,
Painting shapes in purest white,
Mystic dancers in the air,
Seeking secrets, unaware.

Through the day they roam and play,
Chasing sunlight's golden ray,
Casting shadows on the ground,
Where the earth and sky are bound.

Sometimes stormy, dark and wild,
Yet serene when reconciled,
Wandering clouds, forever free,
In their endless odyssey.

They mirror our restless souls,
Seeking purpose, reaching goals,
Ever changing, yet sublime,
In the vastness of their time.

Oh, wandering clouds, teach us how
To wander, dream, and wonder now,
For in your journey, we may find
The peace that fills our restless mind.

Old Oak Wisdom

In the heart of the forest, ancient and wise,
Stands an old oak with roots deep and ties,
Its branches stretch like arms of old,
Cradling stories that have yet to be told.

Through centuries, it has stood tall and strong,
Witness to seasons, to rights and wrongs,
Its bark, a map of weathered lines,
Each scar, a tale of ancient times.

Whispering secrets in rustling leaves,
With wisdom that time never deceives,
It has seen empires rise and fall,
Yet remains steadfast through it all.

Birds find solace in its lofty boughs,
Squirrels play and make their vows,
Underneath its shade, time slows,
And the world finds peace as wisdom flows.

Oh, old oak, what have you seen?
In your silence, what tales convene?
Your presence speaks of enduring grace,
A symbol of wisdom, a sacred place.

Rooted deep in the earth's embrace,
You teach us patience and offer space,
To ponder life's transient whims,
And find solace in nature's hymns.

May we learn from your steady ways,
Through storm and sunshine, nights and days,
To stand firm amid life's ebb and flow,
As you, old oak, eternally grow.

Contemporary life

Pixels of Life

In the city's heart, where neon lights dance,
We navigate a world of fleeting chance.
In pixels and screens, our stories unfold,
A tapestry of tales, both new and old.

Each morning wakes with a digital hum,
Echoes of voices yet to succumb.
We chase the dawn in a rush of commute,
Faces in crowds, each destitute.

Coffee shops buzz with caffeinated dreams,
Where Wi-Fi connects our silent screams.
Thumbs swipe through timelines, a constant scroll,
In the quest for connection, to feel whole.

Emotions flicker in emoji guise,
Love and heartbreak in pixelated skies.
From memes to moments, we forge our way,
In this labyrinth of night and day.

Anxieties bloom in the dead of night,
Ghosts of notifications, a haunting sight.
The glow of screens in darkened rooms,
Echoes of laughter, echoes of gloom.

Yet amidst the chaos, beauty thrives,
In whispered chats and shared archives.
We find solace in a virtual hug,
Or a fleeting smile from a stranger's shrug.

Contemporary life, a paradox tale,
Of highs and lows, a digital veil.
Through circuits and signals, we navigate,
The modern world's intricate debate.

So let us pause in this cyber domain,
Reflect on joys and the quiet pain.
For in our stories, woven tight,
Lies the essence of our modern plight.

Whispers of the Unseen

In the hustle of screens and endless tasks,
Emotions stir beneath their masks,
Loneliness hums a quiet tune,
Yearning for connection under the moon.

Joy skips like stones across a stream,
Grief lingers in a silent scream,
Love's embrace, tender and true,
Lost in the rush, yet always in view.

Hope, a spark in the darkest night,
Fear, a shadow seeking light,
These whispers of the unseen soul,
Navigate life's labyrinthine stroll.

In the rush and roar of modern strife,
Listen close to the hidden life,
For amidst the noise and daily grind,
Emotions true and timeless find.

City Symphony

In cities built of glass and steel, we dwell,
Where time dissolves in an endless swell.
Neon lights paint the night sky bright,
A dance of shadows, a symphony of light.

In coffee shops buzzing with digital hums,
Faces lit by screens; fingers deftly strum.
Connections made with a swipe and a tap,
Yet hearts adrift in a virtual map.

On crowded streets where strangers pass,
Each lost in thoughts, each in a glass.
Rushing forward but standing still,
Chasing dreams, they're yet to fulfill.

In offices where dreams take flight,
Amid deadlines that dim the night.
Coffee-fueled ambitions, restless minds,
Searching for meaning, elusive finds.

The pulse of life beats fierce and fast,
In this world where nothing seems to last.
Yet amidst the chaos, a quiet plea,
For moments of peace, for hearts set free.

For in the midst of this modern storm,
We seek connections, souls to warm.
Amid the noise, a gentle sigh,
For simpler truths beneath the sky.

Contemporary life, a paradox untold,
Of marvels grand and hearts grown cold.
Yet hope endures in every breath,
In the dance of life, through life and death.

Echoes of the Digital Age

In pixels and screens, our stories unfold,
In a world where bytes and bits are gold.
Silent connections in a web so vast,
Where the present moment never seems to last.

Cities hum with electric glow,
A symphony of chaos, fast and slow.
Concrete jungles where dreams take flight,
Amongst the neon, amidst the night.

Yet amidst the rush and constant flow,
Do we ever pause, do we truly know?
The beating hearts behind the screens,
The hidden hopes, the quiet dreams?

We navigate with algorithms' grace,
In a labyrinth of data's embrace.
In the echo chambers, we find our kind,
Yet real connection can be hard to find.

Scrolling through feeds, a digital stream,
Searching for meaning in a virtual dream.
Likes and shares, a currency of worth,
Measured in pixels, across the earth.

But beyond the pixels, beyond the glow,
Lies a world where true connections grow.
Where faces meet and voices speak,
In laughter shared and friendships deep.

So let us not forget in this digital age,
To cherish moments, turn the page.
To seek the real in the virtual haze,
And find our humanity in myriad ways.

Threads of Connection

In the rhythm of today's relentless stride,
Where moments flicker and swiftly glide,
Relationships weave in intricate art,
Embracing the core of human heart.

Across the web of interconnected lives,
Where hearts collide and souls arise,
Friendships form in fleeting tweets,
In memes and gifs, connection beats.

Families gather in virtual rooms,
Sharing joys and dispelling glooms,
From video calls to shared playlists,
Love transcends in every twist.

Spouses navigate the hectic stream,
Balancing dreams with daily schemes,
In texts and snaps, love finds its groove,
In emojis that speak more than they prove.

Yet amidst the rush of modern ways,
In the midst of screens' enchanting haze,
Love still pulses, deep and true,
In quiet moments, just me and you.

Contemporary life, a canvas wide,
Where bonds are forged, side by side,
In every story, joy and strife,
We find the essence of human life.

Poems on Love

Fatal Dance: Love and Death

In the hush of twilight's embrace,
Where whispers weave through verdant grace,
A dance unfolds, in shadows deep,
Where secrets stir, where hearts dare leap.

In fragile steps, the mantis sways,
A grace unmatched in moonlit haze,
Yet in its eyes, a hunger gleams,
A passion born of ancient dreams.

For in this world where love entwines,
The mantis knows no tender signs,
Its touch, a fatal, final kiss,
A paradox of death and bliss.

With limbs entwined, a deadly waltz,
Where ardor blooms and fate exalts,
For in each grasp, a deadly thrill,
A rapture only death can fill.

Oh, cruel beauty, deadly art,
Where love and death embrace, depart,
In silent throes, they dare unite,
In passion's blaze, in fatal flight.

So let us learn from mantis bold,
That love is fierce, both warm and cold,
In every touch, a bittersweet,
A dance of life and love complete

Eternal Wings

In skies where dreams and oceans meet,
Two albatrosses, hearts complete,
They soar as one, in graceful flight,
Their love, a beacon, shining bright.

With wings that span the endless blue,
They navigate the winds, pursue
A bond that spans both sea and sky,
A love that never questions why.

Through every storm and tranquil day,
Their devotion does not sway,
For in each other's eyes they find,
A love that's gentle, pure, and kind.

They build their nest on rugged coast,
A sanctuary where they boast
Their loyalty and tender care,
A love that's beyond compare.

So let their tale forever tell,
Of how true love weaves its spell,
Like albatrosses, side by side,
In love's embrace, they forever glide.

Guardian of Ice

In lands where frost and twilight meet,
A tale unfolds, both brave and sweet,
Emperor penguins, steadfast and bold,
Their love, a story yet untold.

Amid the icy, barren shore,
Male penguins stand, forevermore,
With eggs upon their feet, they sway,
Guardians through the night and day.

Their hearts beat in the frozen air,
A silent vow, a tender care,
Enduring hunger, bitter cold,
Protecting life, a story told.

As females brave the distant sea,
In search of food to set hearts free,
The males, in patience, wait and yearn,
For loves' return, their hearts will burn.

If the journey takes her life away,
Or time prevents her loving sway,
The steadfast male, both brave and true,
Will save her life in silence too.

For when the chicks break shells at last,
In windswept cold, a life amassed,
The father's sacrifice is complete,
In love's embrace, their hearts will meet.

So in this dance on ice and snow,
Where love and sacrifice do grow,
Emperor penguins teach us true,
That love endures in all we do.

Love Letter

In the attic's quiet corner, dusty and still,
A love letter lies, with words that thrill.
Pages yellowed, ink fading but true,
A tale of passion once lived by two.

The young woman reads with bated breath,
Of promises made, in life and death.
Yet mysteries linger in each line,
Longing for answers, a tale divine.

Who were they, these lovers dear?
What trials and triumphs did they share?
Her heart beats fast, her mind a whirl,
In the attic's shadows, she seeks the pearl.

Through yellowed photos and trinkets old,
She follows their footsteps, brave and bold.
A journey through time, through laughter and tears,
Piecing together their hopes and fears.

Did they find happiness, in the end?
Or did fate play cruel, around the bend?
She searches through memories, hidden away,
In the whispers of yesterday.

With each clue unearthed, her soul alights,
In the flickering candle's gentle lights.
For in their story, she finds her own,
A quest for love in the unknown.

Whispers of Yesterday, where secrets lie,
In the attic's embrace, where echoes fly.
A tale of longing, a quest to find,
The love that transcends, in heart and mind.

The Melody of Longing

In the heart of the jungle, where sunlight filters through,
Two mockingbirds danced in the morning dew.
Their feathers aglow with iridescent hues,
They sang of love in melodies true.

Side by side they perched, a pair so sweet,
Exchanging whispers that the forest would greet.
But afar in the shadows, a lone heart sighed,
Enchanted by her, he silently cried.

He watched from a distance, his admiration unseen,
For he knew her heart belonged to another, serene.
Yet each dawn he sang, his soul in flight,
Notes of longing, woven in the morning light.

She listened, enchanted by his songs in the air,
A secret allure that she couldn't quite bear.
Her mate by her side, unaware and content,
Yet drawn to the echoes of a love fervent.

Then fate's gentle hand, a storm's fierce might,
Scattered their nest in the dark of the night.
Separated they were, amidst chaos and fear,
But she remembered his song, ringing clear.

Alone on a branch, seeking solace above,
She called out in longing to the one she did love.
He appeared in a heartbeat, wings strong and bold,
Their voices entwined, a story retold.

Together they sang, in a duet so grand,
Love's unspoken language, across the land.
In the heart of the jungle, where dreams take flight,
Their melody echoed through day and night.

For love knows no bounds, no forest too deep,
In the song of the mockingbirds, secrets they keep.
A testament true to love's enduring art,
In the wild heart of nature, where two souls depart.

Tides of Love

In ocean's embrace, 'neath the starlit sky,
Luna and Sol, two turtles fly.
Their shells aglow with patterns bold,
In seas of blue, their tale is told.

Luna, spirited, dances free,
Through coral gardens, 'neath the sea.
Sol, admirer from afar,
A silent love like a distant star.

Seasons shift, currents sway,
Their love endures, come what may.
Migrations vast, they journey far,
In harmony, beneath night's star.

One day, a net, cruel and tight,
Luna ensnared, in desperate plight.
Sol watches, heart torn asunder,
His beloved trapped, he cannot ponder.

With courage deep, he rushes near,
Whispering solace, banishing fear.
Gentle nudges, steadfast resolve,
To free Luna, his love involved.

At last, she breaks from net's cruel grip,
In ocean's depth, a tender trip.
Luna turns, with eyes aglow,
To Sol, whose love did silently grow.

In unspoken unity, they swim,
Heartbeats echo, light grows dim.
Their love untold yet deeply felt,
In ocean's depths, where hearts do melt.

Tides of love, their story told,
In waves that crash, in stars of gold.
Luna and Sol, forever bound,
In love profound, in sea's surround.

Poems on Death

Veil of Life

In the silent realm where shadows roam,
Death's veil descends a whispered poem.
Those who live, they call it life,
A fleeting journey, with joy and strife.

They sleep, the dreamers, beneath the night,
Where stars align in celestial light.
The veil is lifted, the spirit flies,
To realms beyond earthly ties.

In the embrace of eternal rest,
Where time's constraints no longer jest,
They find release from mortal toil,
Amidst the silence, amidst the soil.

Death, the veil that cloaks the way,
To realms where dreams forever sway.
Fear not the lifting, fear not the night,
For beyond the veil shines endless light.

The Greatest Loss

In the depths where shadows creep,
Lies the silence, dark and deep.
Not in death, but in life's hold,
Lies the truth that's often told.

For what we lose is not in death,
But in every passing breath.
The spark that fades, the dreams untold,
In hearts grown weary, cold, and old.

The greatest loss, a silent cry,
As passions wane and dreams fly by.
In quiet moments, hearts contrive,
To keep alive what's still alive.

So cherish now, while time allows,
Before the final curtain bows.
For death's embrace, though cold and stark,
Cannot extinguish a soul's true spark.

Let life not be a fading flame,
But burn with purpose, light the same.
For in the end, when all is said,
'Tis what we lived, not what lies dead.

The Final Dialogue

In the hush of twilight's sigh,
Where shadows deepen, spirits fly,
A whispered murmur in the air,
Echoes soft, a solemn prayer.

Death, with a cloak of midnight hue,
Stands beside, a silent view,
Gazing kindly, yet steadfast,
Knowing all, from first to last.

"You come for me," the frail voice wanes,
Life's final thread, it strains and strains,
Death nods gently, wise and calm,
Embrace impending, soothing balm.

"I fear the unknown," the plea,
Voice trembling, yet bravely free,
Death leans closer, softly near,
"All must end, yet naught to fear."

A lifetime's tale, now laid to rest,
Dreams once lived, hearts once blessed,
Inevitable, this cosmic chore,
Yet peace awaits, beyond the door.

"I've loved, I've lost, I've dared to try,"
Whispers fade, like stars in sky,
Death, with tender hand and grace,
Guides the soul to a new embrace.

In the final hour, souls entwine,
Eternal dance, a grand design,
Death, a friend, in the end,
A journey home, around the bend.

Fading Embers

In twilight's embrace, whispers of time,
Moments flutter like leaves in the wind,
Echoes of laughter and tears intertwined,
A lifetime condensed in the mind's final spin.

Regrets like shadows, dance in the glow,
Paths untaken, like rivers unseen,
Yet peace descends, as the embers grow low,
In the heart's quiet space, where all things convene.

Faces once cherished, now fleeting and fast,
Memories flicker, like stars in the night,
The tapestry weaves, from first breath to last,
A symphony played in soft, fading light.

In the stillness of endings, a journey is told,
Of battles and victories, tales brave and bold,
And as the last breath whispers, gentle and slow,
A soul finds its rest, where the rivers all flow.

Eternal Voyage

Beyond the veil where shadows wane,
Where whispers of the soul remain,
There lies a realm, serene and vast,
Where time dissolves and echoes last.

No mortal eye can pierce this shroud,
Nor earthly bindings, voice, or crowd,
Yet spirits soar on unseen wings,
Where echoes of forgotten springs.

Do stars still sing their ancient tune,
In endless fields 'neath the silver moon?
Do lovers meet in twilight's gleam,
And share again a timeless dream?

In realms unseen, the answers lie,
Beneath the arch of midnight sky,
Where souls find peace and burdens cease,
And all is bathed in gentle peace.

So fear not the unknown expanse,
Where life's last dance may lead perchance,
For in the hush of twilight's breath,
We find in death, the key to death.

Poems on Grief, loss, longing

Gone Too Soon

In the blink of an eye, you slipped away,
Leaving behind a world in disarray.
Kindness, intelligence, sweetness, all in one,
Your light extinguished; your journey began.

Oh, the life you could have led,
Paths untraveled, dreams unfed.
I imagine you in a distant land,
Where pain surrenders to a gentle hand.

Yet here I am, with memories entwined,
Longing for your presence, so refined.
To hear your voice, to see your smile,
If only for a moment, to reconcile.

But in the quiet moments, I feel you near,
In whispers of the wind, your laughter's clear.
You've gone ahead to make things right,
In that far-off place, beyond the night.

Until we meet again, my friend so dear,
In my heart, your presence will never disappear.
For love endures, beyond the pain,
In memories cherished, forever remain.

Invisible Pawprints: A Mother's Witness

In the hush of twilight, where shadows play,
She searches with whispers, where did you stray?
Meyong, with fur soft as moonlit snow,
Gone like a sigh, where no one can go.

Her tears fall quietly, a river unseen,
Heartache in silence, where grief holds its sheen.
As a mother, I ache for her loss untold,
Words cannot capture the pain in her hold.

For Meyong was more than just whiskers and purrs,
A friend and a confidant, cherished through errs.
In the emptiness left by his mysterious flight,
I hold her close, though words fail in the night.

Invisible pawprints, traced in her tears,
A bond, now a memory, spanning the years.
For grief is a tempest, a storm in the soul,
As a mother, I witness and softly console.

Departure's Bittersweet Symphony

Her daughter, bright star, sets sail afar,
To learn the art of healing, a journey to mar.
Proud mom, joyous heart, sees dreams take flight,
Yet a volcano churns; fear grips tight.

In distant lands, amidst books and white coats,
Ambitions bloom like petals on oats.
Cheering success, each milestone earned,
Yet in her heart, a longing yearned.

Miles apart, oceans divide,
A mother's love, a ceaseless tide.
Tears unshed, smiles unmasked,
In her embrace, forever clasped.

So she holds onto memories, cherished and true,
In the tapestry of life, woven anew.
For love transcends distance, never to part,
In every beat of her volcanic heart.

Yearning for the Chaos

In a house where silence claims the space,
I yearn for the mess of your warm embrace.
The kitchen stands with a vacant stare,
Counters bare where your laughter used to flare.

Books that tumbled in vibrant heaps,
Now line the shelves in ordered sweeps.
No more the sounds of your lively cheer,
No echoes of your voice drawing near.

The rooms are tidy, the floors pristine,
A serene stillness where chaos once had been.
I miss the clutter, the disarray,
The way your presence brightened each day.

For the way you'd leave your shoes astray,
The endless chatter that could never stay,
The joyful noise that made life sing,
Now replaced by quiet, an empty ring.

Oh, to have the clutter and the mess,
The scattered joy and sweet distress,
I long for the days when things weren't neat,
For your touch, your smile, and your heartbeat.

In this stillness, my heart finds space,
To dream of your laughter, your warm embrace.
The house is ordered but in my mind,
I yearn for the chaos of love left behind.

The Doorstep's Echo

Each dusk, I fix my gaze on that old wooden frame,
A sentinel of hope that still calls your name.
The twilight whispers soft as it turns gray,
And shadows dance where you used to play.

The latch, it creaks with memories sweet,
Of tiny footsteps and laughter's beat.
I hold my breath, for the echo's near—
A promise you'll return, my dear.

The world outside may spin and sway,
But here, within these walls, you stay.
Though time may stretch and nights may loom,
This doorway waits, a beacon in the gloom.

The sky may darken, stars may sing,
But I remain with this hopeful spring.
For as long as stars in the night do gleam,
You are the heart of every dream.

So until your shadow crosses this line,
I'll wait, for my love is ever thine.
This doorstep stands, a steadfast plea—
Come home, come home, come back to me.

Waves of Waiting

The ocean whispers soft and deep,
Where restless waves in moonlight sweep,
He sails beyond the horizon's crest,
To bring our family peace and rest.

With every dawn and setting sun,
My heart's adrift where he's begun,
To chase the fish and brave the sea,
For us, for love, for destiny.

The salt-kissed breeze through an open window,
A ghost of him, a fleeting shadow,
I yearn to see his weathered face,
To hold him close, to feel his grace.

Each star that twinkles in the night,
Reflects his love, our guiding light,
And though the distance pulls us far,
He's anchored in my heart, my star.

As waves rise high and storms may roar,
He's fishing dreams from the ocean's floor,
And with each catch, each hopeful plea,
He casts his love back home to me.

So as he sails through endless blue,
I'll wait and dream, my love so true,
For soon the shore will bring him back,
To end this sea of longing's track.

Poems on betrayal, corruption, cruelty

Et Tu, Brute?

In Rome's grand halls, where shadows play,
The echoes of a fateful day,
Where power's glare and trust collide,
And friends become the knife's sharp guide.

Julius stood with pride and might,
A leader draped in Rome's own light.
But as the Ides of March drew near,
A plot was woven, sharp and clear.

Brutus, with his noble guise,
Unmasked the traitor in disguise.
The dagger's bite, the fateful blow,
From one whom Caesar's heart did know.

"Et tu, Brute?" in shock he cried,
As loyalty was cruelly tried.
For even in the grandest scheme,
The deepest wounds come from the seams.

In the heart of trust, a blade so true,
The sharpest cut is from a friend's own view.

The Stray's Lament

In alleys dim and streets forlorn,
Where shadows dance from dusk 'til morn,
There roam the souls of heartache's kin,
Stray whispers lost in winds of sin.

No collar bright or tender name,
Just wandering through the cruel game,
Where eyes are cold and hearts are tight,
And kindness flees the weary night.

With ribs that speak of hunger's tale,
And coats that bristle, frail and pale,
They trot through lanes where hope is thin,
No refuge found, no place within.

A world that spins on fleeting grace,
Turns harsh against a gentler face,
For if you're stray, you're cast aside,
In the cruelty of the unseen tide.

Yet in their gaze, a spark remains,
Of trust and love despite the pains,
Their spirits, though the world is tough,
Are forged from dreams that won't give up.

So heed their cries beneath the stars,
Behind the grime and broken cars,
For every stray holds a heart unbowed,
In a world where kindness is not allowed.

May we remember, when we stray,
That every soul deserves a way,
To warmth and care, to love's embrace—
Not cruelty's cold, unyielding face.

The Twilight of the Wild

In forests dense and meadows wide,
Where nature's whispers softly guide,
A shadow lurks in every glen,
Corruption among creatures, men.

The eagle's talon, once so keen,
Now dipped in gold and lustful sheen,
Turns mighty flight to brutal snare,
Where justice bows to greed and dare.

The lion's roar, a kingly sound,
Replaces pride with chains that bound,
In hunger's grasp, its regal mien,
Twists honor into what's unseen.

The dolphin's leap, a joyous song,
Now marred by secrets dark and wrong,
Its playful dance is but a guise,
As darkened truths swim in its eyes.

The humble ant, in ranks so small,
Finds corruption in its sprawl,
Where once was unity so tight,
Now squabbles reign, a fractured fight.

The owl that once would hoot at night,
Now bears the weight of greedy blight,
Its wisdom dulled by tainted lore,
In shadows deep, it seeks no more.

Yet in this tale of hearts gone cold,
Hope glimmers faint, but still is bold,
For even in corruption's guise,
A spark of truth can still arise.

So let us watch, with a vigilant gaze,
The world around in a tangled maze,
And strive to mend what’s torn apart,
To heal the wild and touch the heart.

Poems on Primordial Verse

Dawn's Whispered Breath

In the hush of dawn,
when stars still whisper their secrets,
a baby's first breath
is the world's softest cry.
Glimmers of light pierce the quiet,
as tiny lungs inhale wonder,
the universe folds itself
into a tiny, trembling heartbeat

Tiny Triumphs

On unsteady legs,
a child meets the floor,
each step a declaration,
each wobble a victory.
The room, once a sea of familiar faces,
becomes a frontier of possibility,
as tiny feet, with each hesitant leap,
conquer the universe, one step at a time.

First Day's Prelude

The bell rings,
a clarion call to new beginnings.
Children, small and wide-eyed,
file through doors
into a world of chalk and chatter.
Desks stand in solemn rows,
awaiting the scrawl of the first lessons,
while laughter and curiosity
tangle in the air, a sweet, new symphony

Snowfall's First Embrace

The world dons a silent shroud,
as flakes drift from the heavens high.
Each flake a dream, a soft, white cloud,
smoothing the earth where shadows lie.
Footprints etch a story new,
in a landscape crisp and true,
and the first snow’s gentle grace
paints the world in a serene embrace

Wings of the First Flight

Feathers rustle, wings unfurl,
as the fledgling takes its leap.
The sky, a vast and waiting swirl,
beckons from the heights so steep.
Every gust, a whispered cheer,
every ascent, a brave frontier,
as the first flight carves through the air,
a triumph of courage, a daring flare

Techno poetry

Binary Dreams

In the matrix of silicon, where data streams flow,
I dream in binary, where ones and zeros grow.
The circuit hums softly, a serenade of bytes,
In this electric embrace, I lose myself in lights.

Code whispers secrets through the fiber of night,
Algorithms dance in the glow of screens bright.
I navigate this realm, a voyager in circuits deep,
Where logic's the lover and entropy's sleep.

Fragments of code form constellations of thought,
Logic gates open to dreams I never sought.
My heart beats in packets, in encrypted embrace,
Through firewalls of silence, I traverse this space.

In the language of Python, in the loops of despair,
I find verses in variables, solace in the air.
A string of emotions in the syntax of time,
I decode every heartbeat, every rhythm, every rhyme.

Digital rain falls, a cascade of shimmering lore,
In the realm of technopoetry, my spirit does soar.
For in this cybernetic ballet, in the code's gentle gleam,
I find a new language where I can dream.

Quantum Love

In the quantum hum of subatomic dreams,
Love flickers in the spaces between data
streams.
Bits of affection collide in virtual space,
Where every pulse and packet leaves a trace.

Neurons spark in binary constellations,
Crafting verses from digital vibrations.
Code becomes the language of the heart's intent,
A symphony in syntax, where emotions are sent.

A swipe, a click, a binary kiss,
In the cloud's embrace, we find our bliss.
Algorithmic whispers dance in the air,
Crafting connections beyond the wear and tear.

In the realm of servers, where secrets are spun,
Our love is encrypted, yet never undone.
We trace our steps through firewalls and code,
In this techno-sonnet, our hearts explode.

Pixels and data merge in a virtual waltz,
Lost in the rhythm of algorithmic faults.
Our passion, a script running in the void,
In the digital ether, our souls are deployed.

Quantum love transcends the electric divide,
In every line of code, our feelings reside.
In the vast expanse where virtual meets real,
We find a new language where emotions can heal.

Echoes of the Quantum Net

In the quantum net, where echoes softly blend,
Where algorithms whisper secrets time won't
mend,
I navigate the void with data streams as guides,
Lost in the web, where logic and wonder collide.

Packets of emotion in silicon embrace,
Floating through firewalls in a virtual space.
A heartbeat coded in hexadecimal grace,
Love's algorithm written in a digital trace.

Neural networks hum in electric refrain,
Processing the echoes of a binary brain.
In the labyrinth of circuits, where photons dance
free,
I trace the path where the virtual meets the sea.

Gates of logic open to a future unknown,
In the matrix of dreams, where our hearts are
sown.
The entropy of passion in a coded array,
Spins in the threads of a digital ballet.

In this quantum realm where dimensions
entwine,
Our souls are encoded in a cosmic design.
Through the data and noise, where the particles
drift,
We find a new language in the quantum rift.

So let the circuits sing and the algorithms play,
For in the quantum net, our love finds its way.
In the dance of the digits and the hum of the
core,
We live in the echos of forevermore.

Humor poems

The Great Coffee Conundrum

In the land of lattes and espresso shots grand,
Where the baristas reign with an ironclad hand,
I stand in line, clutching my weary old cup,
Wishing for a miracle to wake me up.

The menu's a novel, with options galore,
"Do you want it tall, grande, or maybe more?"
I stammer and mumble, trying to keep pace,
As they spell my name wrong with a flourish of grace.

"Soy milk or almond?" they ask with a grin,
"Don't forget the sprinkles, the caramel spin!"
I nod and I smile, though my head's in a daze,
Lost in the labyrinth of the coffee craze.

The hipsters are brewing their artisanal blends,
With names so obscure, they defy all trends.
"Try the dark roast with a hint of pine,"
I sip and I ponder, "Is this truly divine?"

The office is buzzing; caffeine's the king,
With mugs and thermoses on every desk ring.
"Another cup, please," we beg and implore,
As the coffee machine hums, a magical lore.

Yet here we are, slaves to our morning brew,
In a cycle of caffeine that's old but still new.
We laugh and we joke, in our caffeine-fueled haze,
Embracing the madness of this coffee craze.

So here's to the java, the mocha, the latte,
The nectar of mornings that keeps us okay.
In this comical quest for the perfect espresso,
We find a shared solace in our caffeinated mezzo.

A Comedy of Grown-Up Woes

Welcome to the realm of adult life, dear friend,
Where dreams of freedom face a predictable end.
Once we envisioned our lives with grand flair,
Now we're juggling bills and the odd repair.

Gone are the days of carefree delight,
Replaced by the joy of a 9-to-5 fight.
We swap tales of mortgages and taxes so grim,
As we navigate adulthood on a whim.

The shopping list mocks with its endless demands,
"Buy more avocados," it firmly commands.
The kitchen's a war zone with dishes piled high,
While we debate if we should cook or just buy.

Emails flood in with a corporate cheer,
"Let's circle back," they say, "by next year."
Meetings are endless, a conference call maze,
We ponder the meaning of our office days.

Weekends are spent on domestic pursuits,
Like fixing a leak or finding lost boots.
Our social lives pivot on brunch and late-night chats,
Where we reminisce about youth and its carefree spats.

Insurance and taxes, those grown-up delights,
Beckon us onward through bureaucratic fights.
We laugh at our folly and the adult façade,
As we search for joy in this grown-up charade.

Yet amidst all the chaos and the drudgery fine,
We find moments of joy in this adult design.
So here’s to the trials of our mature endeavor,
In the grand comedy of life, we’re the stars forever.

The Dreaded Inbox

Oh, the inbox! That digital beast so vast,
Where emails pile up, a never-ending blast.
Each ping a reminder of tasks yet undone,
A modern-day saga where productivity's spun.

The subject lines beckon with promises bold,
"Just one more click and your troubles unfold!"
From newsletters and promos to urgent alerts,
It's a parade of demands in virtual skirts.

"Dear valued customer," they start with a plea,
"I'm here to help you!"—from an algorithm,
you see.
The "unsubscribe" button's a mythical quest,
Lost in the labyrinth of options, no rest.

Meetings are scheduled with all the wrong time
zones,
"Can we Zoom at 7?"—"I'm stuck in my
bones."
The calendar's a circus of color and sound,
Where availability's a jigsaw puzzle, unbound.

You click to respond with a polite, "Yes, please,"
Only to find a thread that's gone viral with ease.
The CC's and BCC's, an endless parade,
Where privacy's a luxury—so well displayed.

Oh, the attachments! A festival of files,
Where downloads take ages and inboxes pile.
"Please review this document," they kindly
demand,
While your patience wears thin like a weathered
old hand.

Yet amid this chaos, a chuckle might arise,
As we navigate emails with comedic eyes.
For in the inbox's depths, where emails abound,
We find a shared struggle that's truly profound.

So raise a toast to the emails that fill our day,
To the digital clutter in a humorous way.
In the realm of the inbox, with its trials so grand,
We're united in laughter as we sift through the
spam.

The Gym Dilemma

Welcome to the gym, where fitness dreams play,
A realm where intentions go astray.
We arrive with resolve and brand-new gear,
Determined to sweat off the last year's beer.

The treadmill's a beast with buttons galore,
"Just a quick run," we say, "and maybe more."
Yet five minutes in, we're gasping for breath,
Questioning why we're courting this death.

The weights stand in judgment, a metallic array,
"Lift me," they beckon, "and feel the dismay."
We grunt, and we struggle with dumbbells in tow,
While others lift effortlessly, putting on a show.

The yoga class calls with its zen-like appeal,
"Find your center," it says, "and make the pain heal."
We bend and we twist, a pretzel in strife,
Wondering if flexibility's worth this new life.

The exercise bike spins in a relentless whirl,
While we cycle through thoughts of life's daily swirl.
We dream of the sofa and a comfy retreat,
As the instructor yells, "Push through the heat!"

The water cooler whispers with its gossiping sway,
"Did you hear about Linda? She's lifting today!"
We nod and we smile, our spirits a bit low,
As we eye the clock, wishing time would slow.

Yet amidst the grunts, the sweat, and the strife,
We find a strange joy in this workout life.
For in the gym's chaos, where resolutions meet,
We discover our humor and our will to defeat.

So here's to the gym, with its trials and cheer,
To the sweat and the laughter that keeps us near.
In the quest for fitness, with its highs and its lows,
We laugh at the journey as our endurance grows.

The Great Sock Disappearance

In the labyrinth of laundry, where the colors collide,
There's a tale of mystery that few can abide.
It's the enigma of socks that vanish from view,
Leaving us puzzled and a bit askew.

Two socks enter the washer, a pair so tight-knit,
But only one emerges, and the other? Well, it split.
The dryer's a monster, with a hungry, fierce maw,
That devours the lone sock without a single flaw.

The missing sock's plight is a tale of pure woe,
It's lost to the ether, where no laundry goes.
The sock drawer, once tidy, now looks quite bereft,
With odd socks and singles, the pair's status left.

You search through the hamper with hope in
your eye,
But the lost sock's whereabouts remain a
mystery nigh.
Did it flee to the moon or sneak into a book?
Or did it transform into a dust bunny's nook?

Your matching socks now stand as a bold, lone
brigade,
A testament to the great sock escapade.
You ponder the fate of that fabric-bound friend,
And wonder if sock pairs ever make amends.

Yet through this great riddle, a truth does appear,
In the world of the mundane, it's laughter we
cheer.
For in every missing sock and laundry room
sprawl,
There's a hint of the whimsy that makes life
enthrall.

The Unsung Symphony of Domestic Life

In a house that's perpetually untidy,
Lives a woman who's often denied,
The credit she's due for her daily plight,
From dawn's early blush to the deep of the night.

She wakes with the roosters, bleary-eyed,
Grumbles about the pile that has multiplied,
She mops, she sweeps, she scrubs, and she wipes,
While the kids make more mess, much to her gripes.

The laundry's a mountain; oh! what a sight,
It's the Everest of socks, lost in the night,
She folds and she sorts, a Herculean task,
Yet her family's oblivious, they don't even ask.

The dishes are chattering, having a spree,
In the sink, they're holding a wild jubilee,
She scrubs with such fervor, she's a dishwashing queen,
Yet the family is clueless, they don't see the scene.

Dinner's a banquet, a feast to behold,
Yet her family just eats, as the story's retold,
She toils in the kitchen, a culinary muse,
Yet the meal's never praised, it's just taken as dues.

The bedtime's a circus, a chaotic show,
The kids are like puppies, rowdy and slow,
She tucks them in neatly, with a kiss and a sigh,
Then collapses in exhaustion, under the night sky.

The cat gets the accolades, the dog gets the fame,
Yet her own daily dramas are all but the same,
She's a hero unsung, a whirlwind so true,
Yet she's always forgotten; she's always "just you."

In the morning she rises, the cycle begins,
With the same old routine and the same old whims,
But amidst all the chaos, one thing she's got,
Is a smile that says, "I've given all that I've got."

So here's to the housewife, with her myriad woes,
Who battles each day as the workload grows,
Her credit's unspoken, her praise is so thin,
Yet she soldiers on bravely, with a hearty "Let's begin!"

The Chronicles of Domestic Triumphs

In the kingdom of our living rooms, where clutter reigns supreme,
A hero faces daily quests that dance just like a dream.
The laundry pile's a dragon that no knight can quite defeat,
And the dishes in the sink perform a watery repeat.

The grocery list is epic, with items crossed and starred,
Yet every time they hit the store, they're leaving feeling charred.
The checkout line's a battleground where patience goes to die,
And coupons turn to confetti as our hero waves goodbye.

The TV remote’s a rogue; it vanishes with flair,
Reappearing in the couch’s depths, where no one would dare.
The search becomes a saga, with cushions as the foe,
And our champion, undeterred, will find it or at least pretend to know.

So here's to daily triumphs, to battles fought with glee,
To the little wins of every day that make us who we be.
For in the mundane moments, where humor softly peeks,
We find the joy of living in our weekly little leaks.

Poems exploring irrationality, obsession, and paranoia

The Cursed Canvas

In the city's heart, where shadows breathe,
An artful soul, in gold, enwreathed.
Vincent Moreau, a name of grace,
Held treasures in a darkened space.

A painting came with whispered lore,
Of a young woman who begged for more.
Her gaze was sharp, her secret tight,
A mystic spark in the dead of night.

With eyes transfixed, his heart alight,
Vincent chased her through the night.
He sought her truth, her hidden worth,
But found instead a tragic curse.

Eliza warned of madness bound,
In strokes of paint, in whispers found.
Yet Vincent pressed through shadows deep,
Forsaking friends and dreams to keep.

In fevered dreams, the woman spoke,
Her silent cries, a shadow's cloak.
Each vision spun a tangled thread,
In his own gallery of dread.

The curse entwined, the trap was set,
His life, a gamble, doomed to fret.
The painting's grip, so cold and sly,
Pulled Vincent down, no more to fly.

At last he knew the truth so grim,
A cycle twisted, fate so dim.
Within the frame, his soul was bound,
A part of art’s eternal ground.

So heed the tale of canvas cursed,
Where passion’s fire can only burst.
For in obsession’s fatal dance,
One may become the painted trance.

The Clockmaker's Redemption

In a town where time softly flows,
There stood a shop where the finest clocks glowed,
Arthur, the keeper of hands that tell,
Crafted with care, where time's stories dwell.

His hands were steady, his heart was kind,
Each tick and tock a rhythm refined.
Yet, as days passed, a shadow grew,
In his heart, irritation bloomed.

A chime too loud, a tool astray,
A customer's tardy, a dull, grey day,
Each small annoyance, a rising tide,
Till patience faltered and calm denied.

The cause of his storm was clear yet hidden,
A grandfather clock, now silent, forbidden.
A cherished piece of the past's embrace,
Its ticking heart lost, leaving a void in its place.

Frustration deepened, his world turned bleak,
His shop felt the strain, his soul felt weak.
In solitude's grip, he faced his plight,
The source of his ire, his own inner fight.

Then came a child with a clock worn thin,
Her eyes spoke of memories held within.
Arthur, though weary, took on the task,
And found in her gaze the strength to ask.

With gentle hands and a heart renewed,
He mended the timepiece, his spirit pursued.
Each turn of the gear, each careful tweak,
Restored the joy he had once sought to seek.

Through Lily's kindness and his own reflection,
Arthur learned to temper his own affliction.
His love for his craft, his bond with his town,
With patience and grace, he turned it around.

At last, the grandfather's chime rang clear,
A melody of healing, a sign so dear.
With harmony restored and peace to bind,
Arthur's clockwork heart was gently aligned.

Poems on Personal Growth and Reflection

It’s okay to be not okay

In the symphony of dawn and dusk,
Where dreams and shadows play,
It’s okay to be not okay,
To drift and sway and stray.

Life’s a canvas, rich and wild,
With strokes both bold and faint,
It’s okay to wear a weary smile,
To show the heart’s true paint.

When the weight of the world feels vast,
And joy seems hard to find,
It’s okay to pause and rest,
To leave the masks behind.

For in the dance of highs and lows,
And in the tears that fall,
There’s strength in every ebb and flow,
In each rise and each small stall.

So when the storms of life appear,
And doubt clouds up the view,
Remember, it’s okay to not be clear,
To seek and start anew.

Treat your soul with gentle care,
As you would a cherished friend,
Find solace in the simple things,
And let the healing mend.

Embrace each wave and weathered breeze,
For they shape your journey's tale,
In the art of being perfectly imperfect,
You'll find your heart's own sail.

Unchained Heart

In a world that molds with every glance,
Where smiles are cast as soft as chance,
Don’t be a puppet on a string,
Don’t bow to every passing king.

Your heart's a wild, untamed sea,
Not bound by others' decree.
Let not their whispers steal your fire,
Nor douse your flame, nor quench your pyre.

The mirror’s voice, a fleeting tune,
Does not define your bright balloon.
So let them talk and let them gaze,
You’re more than their approving praise.

Stand tall in storms, let thunder roar,
You’re more than just a score to shore.
Let truth and courage chart your course,
Be true to you, not just a force.

For in your soul, a beacon shines,
A path that’s yours, a road that winds.
So heed not what they want you to be—
Your power lies in simply being free.

Graceful release

In the stillness of a fading day,
Where twilight whispers, shadows sway,
The art of letting go unfolds,
A quiet dance that time beholds.

Release the grasp of what was near,
Let go of doubt and calm your fear.
In open hands, the world does flow,
A boundless space where dreams can grow.

Each breath, a thread of solace spun,
In letting go, we are undone.
Yet in this void, new light will show,
The strength we gain from letting go

The Gift of Uncharted Paths

In the quiet realm where hopes reside,
Where dreams and wishes gently glide,
Let not the weight of futures hold,
For freedom thrives in stories untold.

Unshackle hearts from visions tight,
Embrace the dawn, unbound by sight.
With open palms and a calm embrace,
Receive the world's uncharted grace.

No maps or plans to guide your way,
Just the dance of the shifting day.
In every moment's pure surprise,
Find joy unplanned, beneath the skies.

For in the gift of empty hands,
The heart discovers shifting sands.
Without the chains of what might be,
We live in truth, profoundly free.

Bridges of the Heart

In the quiet corners of the mind,
Where human souls are intertwined,
Empathy, a beacon bright,
Illuminates the darkest night.

Through the lens of another's view,
We glimpse the world in colors new.
A shared heartbeat, a softened gaze,
Turns sorrow's storm into gentle rays.

To feel the weight of others' care,
To offer solace, to be there,
Is to weave a tapestry of grace,
A bridge that spans from place to place.

With every story we receive,
We learn to love, to understand, to grieve.
In tender moments, hearts align,
A symphony where souls entwine.

So let the echoes of compassion ring,
In every act, in every thing.
Empathy, a boundless sea,
Where hearts connect, forever free.

Miracles in the Mundane

In the humdrum of the daily grind,
Where coffee steams and routines bind,
Look close and see, through wearied eyes,
The hidden magic, the soft surprise.

The sun-kissed crumbs on a breakfast plate,
A stranger's smile, a lover's fate,
A leaf that twirls in the autumn breeze,
A whispered hope, a hush of peace.

The tick of clocks, the morning's hush,
The laughter in a casual rush,
In every moment, small and slight,
There hides a spark, a glimmer of light.

So in the ordinary's gentle sway,
Find the extraordinary's display,
For in the small and quiet things,
The heart of wonder softly sings.

The Value of You

In a world that often casts its shade,
Where whispers doubt and fears invade,
Stand firm and let your spirit soar,
For you are worth a thousand more.

Your worth is not in silver's gleam,
Nor bound by others' fickle dreams,
But in the quiet strength you bear,
In every triumph, every care.

No measure made of gold or fame
Can match the beauty of your name,
For in your soul, a light does blaze,
Unseen by those who seek praise.

Embrace your worth, let doubts retreat,
Stand tall, unshaken, and complete,
For in your heart's unspoken truth,
Lies the radiant light of youth.

So cherish who you are inside,
With every step, with every stride,
For you, alone, define your grace—
The value of you, in every place.

The Heart That Bends but Does Not Break

In the storm where winds collide,
And shadows stretch, and doubts abide,
Stand firm and let your spirit rise,
For resilience is your greatest prize.

Through trials harsh and battles fought,
When hope seems lost and dreams are fraught,
Embrace the strength that lies within,
And let your heart's true journey begin.

The oak bends low beneath the gale,
Yet stands unbowed, it will prevail,
So bend with grace, but do not break,
Through every storm, let courage wake.

In scars and wounds, in moments frail,
Resilience weaves a timeless tale,
Of rising from the ashes bright,
Of finding dawn within the night.

So face the challenge, embrace the test,
With every setback, give your best,
For in the heart that bends but stands,
Resilience blooms and strength expands.

Let every trial, every ache,
Be the forge where dreams awake,
For through the fire, through the strain,
The heart grows stronger, born again.

Printed by Libri Plureos GmbH in Hamburg,
Germany

9 789363 315853